BASEBALL LEGENDS

Hank Aaron
Grover Cleveland Alexander
Ernie Banks
Johnny Bench
Yogi Berra
Roy Campanella
Roberto Clemente
Ty Cobb
Dizzy Dean
Joe DiMaggio
Bob Feller
Jimmie Foxx
Lou Gehrig
Bob Gibson
Rogers Hornsby
Walter Johnson
Sandy Koufax
Mickey Mantle
Christy Mathewson
Willie Mays
Stan Musial
Satchel Paige
Brooks Robinson
Frank Robinson
Jackie Robinson
Babe Ruth
Duke Snider
Warren Spahn
Willie Stargell
Honus Wagner
Ted Williams
Carl Yastrzemski
Cy Young

CHELSEA HOUSE PUBLISHERS

BASEBALL LEGENDS

JIMMIE FOXX

Norman L. Macht

Introduction by
Jim Murray

Senior Consultant
Earl Weaver

CHELSEA HOUSE PUBLISHERS
New York • Philadelphia

Acknowledgments

This story could not have been told without the generous help of Barbara
Everett, Sudlersville librarian; Joan Marshall of the Sudlersville Community
Betterment Club; Jimmie Foxx's own cousins, Mildred S. Barracliff and Gladys
Truitt; the people who shared their memories of growing up with Foxx: Bernard
Merrick, Ed Walraven, John and Lillian Walraven, Vickers Hollingsworth,
Mildred Stack and Dr. Robert Farr; and Gil Dunn, founder and curator of the
Jimmie Foxx museum on Kent Island, Maryland.

Published by arrangement with
Chelsea House Publishers.
Newfield Publications is a federally
registered trademark of Newfield
Publications, Inc.

Produced by James Charlton Associates
New York, New York.

Designed by Hudson Studio
Ossining, New York.

Typesetting by LinoGraphics
New York, New York.

Picture research by Carolann Hawkins
Cover illustration by Dan O'Leary

Library of Congress Cataloging-in-Publication Data

Macht, Norman L. (Norman Lee), 1929-
    Jimmie Foxx / Norman Macht ; introduction by Jim Murray.
        p.   cm.—(Baseball legends)
    Includes bibliographical references.
    Summary: Examines the life of the baseball player who was active
with several teams, including the Boston Red Sox and the Chicago
Cubs, and was elected to the Baseball Hall of Fame in 1951.
    ISBN o-7910-1175-5.—ISBN 0-7910-1209-3 (pbk.)
    1. Foxx, Jimmie—Juvenile literature. 2. Baseball players—United
States—Biography—Juvenile literature. [1. Foxx, Jimmie.
2. Baseball players.] I. Title. II. Series.
    GV865.F64M33 1990
    796.357'092—dc20
[B]
[92]   90-35388

            CIP

                    AC

CONTENTS

WHAT MAKES A STAR

Jim Murray

No one has ever been able to explain to me the mysterious alchemy that makes one man a .350 hitter and another player, more or less identical in physical makeup, hard put to hit .200. You look at an Al Kaline, who played with the Detroit Tigers from 1953 to 1974. He was pale, stringy, almost poetic-looking. He always seemed to be struggling against a bad case of mononucleosis. But with a bat in his hands, he was King Kong. During his career, he hit 399 home runs, rapped out 3,007 hits, and compiled a .297 batting average.

Form isn't the reason. The first time anybody saw Roberto Clemente step into the batter's box for the Pittsburgh Pirates, the best guess was that Clemente would be back in Double A ball in a week. He had one foot in the bucket and held his bat at an awkward angle—he looked as though he couldn't hit an outside pitch. A lot of other ballplayers may have had a better-looking stance. Yet they never led the National League in hitting in four different years, the way Clemente did.

Not every ballplayer is born with the ability to hit a curveball. Nor is exceptional hand-eye coordination the key to heavy hitting. Big-league locker rooms are filled with players who have all the attributes, save one: discipline. Every baseball man can tell you a story about a pitcher who throws a ball faster than anyone has ever seen but who has no control on or *off* the field.

The Hall of Fame is full of people who transformed themselves into great ballplayers by working at the sport, by studying the game, and making sacrifices. They're overachievers—and winners. If you want to find them, just watch the World Series. Or simply read about New York Yankee great Lou Gehrig; Ted Williams, "the Splendid Splinter" of the Boston Red Sox; or the Dodgers' strikeout king Sandy Koufax.

A pitcher *should* be able to win a lot of ballgames with a 98-miles-per-hour fastball. But what about the pitcher who wins 20 games a year with a fastball so slow that you can catch it with your teeth? Bob Feller of the Cleveland Indians got into the Hall of Fame with a blazing fastball that glowed in the dark. National League star Grover Cleveland Alexander got there with a pitch that took considerably longer to reach the plate; but when it did arrive, the pitch was exactly where Alexander wanted it to be— and the last place the batter expected it to be.

There are probably more players with exceptional ability who didn't make it to the major leagues than there are who did. A number of great hitters, bored with fielding practice, had to be dropped from their team because their home-run production didn't make up for their lapses in the field. And then there are players like Brooks Robinson of the Baltimore Orioles, who made himself into a human vacuum cleaner at third base because he knew that working hard to become an expert fielder would win him a job in the big leagues.

A star is not something that flashes through the sky. That's a comet. Or a meteor. A star is something you can steer ships by. It stays in place and gives off a steady glow; it is fixed, permanent. A star works at being a star.

And that's how you tell a star in baseball. He shows up night after night and takes pride in how brightly he shines. He's Willie Mays running so hard his hat keeps falling off; Ty Cobb sliding to stretch a single into a double; Lou Gehrig, after being fooled in his first two at-bats, belting the next pitch off the light tower because he's taken the time to study the pitcher. Stars never take themselves for granted. That's why they're stars.

1

"THE BEAST"

Hₐis nickname was "The Beast," but he was really a very gentle, good-natured man. And it is a good thing he was, because Jimmie Foxx was one of the strongest men who ever played in the major leagues. Fortunately, the only time he used his strength was to hit baseballs. He hit them harder and farther than any other player of his time, including Babe Ruth, and more than 500 of them were blasted out of ball parks for home runs.

"Foxx hit the ball so far and so often we didn't pay too much attention to most of them," said Bill Werber, a teammate on the Boston Red Sox. "But one I remember was hit in old League Park in Cleveland. It was over 400 feet to the fence, the bleachers extended at least another 50 feet, and on the back of the bleachers was a big billboard advertising Lux soap. The ball went over all of those, over a big white oak tree outside the park, and was still climbing. We all ran out of the dugout to see where it was headed. Outfielder Dusty Cooke turned to me and said, 'It's a lie. I don't believe it.'"

Foxx hit some of the longest home runs ever seen. Of one of his homers, a rival catcher said, "We watched it for two innings."

When Comiskey Park in Chicago was enlarged in 1927 and a second tier of seats was put on the outfield grandstand, the architect boasted that nobody would be able to hit a ball out of that park. But Foxx did it three times. One day in 1936 he launched a rocket that cleared the roof, the street, a parking lot, and a tennis court. A peanut vendor in a room deep under the stands said he heard it clear as a shot.

New York Yankees pitcher Lefty Gomez never forgot what he said was the longest home run ever hit in Yankee Stadium. Gomez threw it. Foxx hit it—all the way into the third tier of the left-field grandstand. And he hit it with so much force it broke the back of a seat near the last row.

During the winter of 1939 there were many arguments over which ball was livelier, the one used in the National League or the one used in the American. One cold day a bunch of players gathered in Baltimore to hit the two balls and see which would carry farther. Foxx hit them both so far he destroyed the experiment.

Jimmie Foxx stood just under 6 feet tall and weighed 185 pounds, not an ounce of it fat.

"He was raw strength," Boston writer Al Hirshberg described him. "He looked like an oak tree at the plate. His feet were planted like roots and his fantastic arms were like branches."

To give his arms room to swing the bat, Foxx cut the sleeves off his uniform just below the shoulder. Other players joked about his broad muscular back, bulging biceps, and powerful forearms.

Lefty Gomez said, "I tried wearing glasses to improve my pitching. The first time I wore them and looked at Foxx, it scared me to death. His arms looked like telephone poles, and every time he squeezed the bat I could see sawdust drip. I threw away the glasses."

Gomez once stood on the mound facing Foxx and shook off every sign catcher Bill Dickey gave him. Finally the catcher walked out to him and said, "You've got to throw something."

"Maybe not," Gomez replied. "If I stand here long enough, maybe he'll get tired of waiting and go away."

None of the jokes bothered Foxx, however. The genial farmboy from Sudlersville, Maryland, had a smile for everybody. Although he was an intense competitor, it was impossible to make him angry. He was never thrown out of a game, never argued with an umpire. Perhaps it was nature's way of protecting the rest of the world, combining "the strength of a gorilla with the disposition of a collie," as one writer described The Beast.

Players and writers also called him Double X, the Maryland Strong Boy, and Foxxie, which was A's manager Connie Mack's name for him. But growing up on the farm, he was always James to his parents and just plain Jim to everybody else in town.

2

FOXX FARM

James Emory Foxx was born on October 22, 1907, in a woodframe farmhouse three miles outside Sudlersville on Maryland's eastern shore. His father, Samuel Dell Foxx, was a tenant farmer. He raised corn to feed his cows, and wheat, paying half his crop to the farm's owner as rent. Mr. Foxx was also a member of the town's baseball team and the best catcher in Queen Annes County. He could have played professionally, but he preferred to stay on the farm. A fiery player, he never backed away from a fight and started more than one himself. Mr. Foxx loved the game more than anything, and when his team was not playing he often umpired for other teams.

Jim's mother, Mattie Smith Foxx, was a large woman, remembered by neighbors as kind and generous. The family names of Foxx and Smith went back a long way in the region; their ancestors had come from England and Ireland at least three generations earlier.

When Jim's name first appeared in local and city newspapers, it was spelled Fox. But, contrary

Young Jim at the age of 12 with his brother Sammy at Tolchester, Maryland.

Like many communities in the early part of the century, Sudlersville had a town baseball team. At age 13, Jimmie (first row, right) was good enough to play with the older teenagers and men.

to some stories, Jim did not change it after he became famous. The family had spelled it with two X's as far back as anyone could remember. It was the Philadelphia writers who began to call him Jimmie, sometimes with a *y* and sometimes with an *ie*. The monument that stands in his home town today reads "Jimmy."

From the time Jim could sit up, his father was always putting a baseball in his hands or rolling one across the tray of his high chair or on the floor.

"Jim was so small it would knock him over," his cousin Gladys Truitt recalled. And another cousin, Mildred Barracliff, added: "Until he was about five, whenever I saw him coming to our house, I'd tell my mother not to let him in until I put all my dolls away. Everything was a ball to him; he'd pick it up and throw it. By the time he was eight he was catching the ball as hard as his father could throw it."

The population of Sudlersville was about 400, mostly farmers and small-business owners. Farm families had very little cash, but there was always more than enough to eat. There was good bass fishing in the nearby Chester River, and quail, duck, and goose could be hunted in winter.

Jim was 15 years old when the first 100-watt electric light bulb was turned on at the lone intersection in town. By the time the power lines and indoor plumbing reached the farm, Jim would already be playing in the big leagues. Until then, the Foxx family used kerosene or acetylene gas lights and carried water in from a well in the yard.

The wood stove in the kitchen glowed with heat every day, all day, winter and summer. In the bedroom over the kitchen, it was cozy and warm on winter nights but uncomfortably hot in the summertime. Jim and his younger brother, Sammy, slept on a soft, puffy mattress stuffed with feathers. When they sank into it, it would fold right over them.

Although some people credit his early life on the farm for developing Jim into baseball's strongest player, Jim's youth was very much like that of millions of farmboys growing up in the second decade of the 20th century. The work days were long. All the Foxxes were up at 4:30 in the morning and busy until dark. From the age of seven, Jim helped milk the cows before breakfast. He then walked about a mile to a one-room grammar school where the teacher taught grades one through six. When he was older, Jim had to walk three miles to a two-room school in the center of town. After school it was time for his afternoon chores. The animals had to be fed and gotten ready for milking again.

In the summer Jim would spell the farmhands out in the fields, plowing behind a horse or cultivating the corn. They had no motorized farm machinery, no sprays to kill the weeds. The soil was turned and the weeds rooted out with a horse-drawn cultivator. In the fall Jim pitched hay into the upper floor of the barn, cut corn, sawed trees into foot-long logs and burst, or split, them into firewood. He loaded 200-pound bags of phosphate onto a wagon, then swung them off at the farm. It was hard work, but Jim was an unusually strong boy. One day a baseball scout stopped to ask directions and Jim picked up the plow in his right hand and pointed with it. Or so the story goes.

Sometimes there were friendly contests of strength. One challenge was to stand in an empty half-bushel basket, feet together with no room to move them, bend down, and lift a 120-pound burlap sack of wheat or corn to your shoulder. Years later, Jim Foxx would take hold of teammate Bill Werber's ankles and lift the 170-pound third baseman straight up off the floor.

Jim's first love was not baseball, though. It was running. The fastest runner in his school, he dreamed of overtaking his idol, Charlie Paddock, the 1920 Olympic gold-medal winner in the 100-yard dash. Paddock was then being called the fastest human alive.

Jim's other ambition was to be an army drummer boy. His grandfather, a Confederate veteran, had filled young Jim's head with stories of courageous drummer boys in the Civil War. When the United States entered World War I in 1917, 10-year old Jim tried to join the army, but they sent him home.

Despite all the hard work, home was often a friendly place to be. On Saturday nights Jim and his friends went into town with their fathers. While the men talked outside the town's three stores, the boys went inside to spend the five cents they had earned for the week. A nickel then was enough to buy a half-pint of ice cream or a big bag of candy. When he could scrape together 25 cents, Jim joined the group that went to the movies in nearby Chestertown. A ticket cost 10 cents; the rest was for candy and a sundae after the show.

On Christmas and New Year's Eve, Jim and a bunch of boys went down to the sawmill and borrowed the big circle-saw blade. They put it on a wagon or held it with an iron rod through the hole and roamed around town banging on it with a hammer.

But the best holiday was the Fourth of July. It featured a parade, a picnic, a horse race, and always a ball game. At the age of 12 Jim was playing on the same team as his father.

3

AN ALL-AROUND ATHLETE

When Jim Foxx was 13 and a freshman in high school, he was 185 pounds of muscle on a 5'11" frame, with the big arms and wrists of a blacksmith. He was a handsome teenager, with a big easy smile and dimples in his chin and left cheek.

Jim was an ordinary student, coping with classes that included English, algebra, geometry, history, Latin, chemistry, agriculture, and shop. When it came to baseball, however, he was truly extraordinary.

The school baseball team had no coach—the boys learned from each other. But Jim, the catcher, already knew a lot about the game.

As Ed Walraven, who played first base, recalled, "I had a two-dollar mitt. Foxx threw so hard my hand was hurting from the first day. It took me until past soccer season before it healed."

And Bernard Merrick, the 95-pound second

Jimmie (kneeling) was captain of his high-school soccer team in 1923.

baseman, had this to say: "Jim could squat down behind home plate and throw to second on a line drive, without getting up. The pitcher had to duck to save his life."

In his junior year, Jim took a turn pitching, but he threw so hard he often knocked the catcher down. And when he came to bat, his line drives were so hard that opposing infielders often ducked instead of trying to catch them.

Jim was a natural all-around athlete. His school had no football team, but he was the captain and center and leading scorer on the basketball squad. He was also captain and center forward on the soccer team. And yet, when the Baltimore sportswriters named him the state's outstanding athlete in 1923, it was for his talents as a track star, not for baseball or basketball. Jim held eight titles in track, including sprints from 50 to 440 yards, the high jump, and the broad jump. Allowed to enter only two events at the state Olympiad, he went out for the high jump and the 220 dash and easily won them both.

Every town had a baseball team in those days, and the rivalries between them were fierce. It was common for towns to hire out-of-town professionals, sometimes even major leaguers, to help them beat an archrival. At the age of 15, Jim earned his first money playing baseball when a team in the next county paid him 5 dollars a game to catch for them. It was the most money he had ever held in his hand.

When the short high-school baseball season ended, a county all-star team was formed to play teams from other states. In 1923, Jim not only caught for the team but played third base and the outfield. At the plate, he batted an impressive .454.

The next year he hit .552 for his school and

Foxx with Frank "Home Run" Baker, the man who discovered Foxx and told Connie Mack about him. As a player, Baker led or tied the American League in home runs four years in a row.

once again was named to the county team. But before the all-stars began their season, Jim received a penny postcard, inviting him to try out with the Easton Farmers. The card was signed by team manager Frank "Home Run" Baker, a former star of the Philadelphia Athletics and New York Yankees.

"I thought somebody was trying to needle me," Foxx later told a reporter. "Maybe a couple of the cutups that hung around the general store in Sudlersville sent it. But when I saw the postmark was Trappe, I decided nobody would go to that much trouble to play a prank."

Jim's power with the bat impressed Baker, who signed the youngster to a contract that paid him $100 a month for four months. That was more money than Jim could have gotten doing anything else, and he thought it would be an exciting way to spend the summer. He did not look at it as anything more than that.

Hundreds of people from the Sudlersville area journeyed to Easton for Jim Foxx's debut on May 31. Though Easton lost the game, Jim gave his fans something to cheer about when he hit a homer out of Federal Park. As it turned out, the Farmers were not much of a team, but 16-year-old Jim was quite a player. Time and again, he rattled the fences with his line drives, and he hit some of the longest home runs ever seen in those parts.

One day Frank Baker went to Shibe Park in Philadelphia to see his two former teams play. Visiting with New York manager Miller Huggins and super-star Babe Ruth before the game, Baker told them all about Foxx and offered to sell him to the Yankees. But the two men just laughed disbelievingly when Baker told them how good a hitter the youngster was.

Baker then walked across the field and told the same story to Connie Mack. "Bake, if he's as good as you say, I'll take him," the Philadelphia manager responded. "Your word is good enough for me." The Athletics paid $2,500 for Jim's contract.

Foxx finished the season at Easton, batting .296 with 10 home runs. The Parksley team won the pennant, however, and went on to face the winners of the Blue Ridge League for the five-state championship. When a Parksley player was injured, Jim was brought in to replace him and hit .391 with 4 home runs in the six-game series.

Minutes after the series ended on September 10th, somebody told Jim there was a telephone call for him. It was Connie Mack: the Athletics were leaving for a western road trip, and he wanted his new player to go with them. Jim protested that he would have to go home and get some clothes, but

Mack told him not to worry; they would find him something to wear. Foxx reported to Philadelphia the very next day.

Connie Mack took an instant liking to the cheerful rookie, although he was surprised to learn that his new player was only 16 years old. Mack kept a close eye on Jim as the train headed for Cleveland, and assigned the veteran catcher Cy Perkins to room with him.

The A's stopped off at Erie, Pennsylvania, to play an exhibition game against the Cincinnati Reds. Foxx was sent in to pinch-hit against the big, crafty lefthander Eppa Rixey, who was old enough to be his father—and came through with a long triple that won the game. It was the only game in which he appeared.

When the A's season ended, Jim returned to Sudlersville and school, still not convinced he had a future in baseball. But then he received a contract for $2,000 and a letter inviting him to spring training with the Athletics in February 1925. Jim's mother wanted him to graduate and go to college, but the prospect of going to Florida in midwinter and playing baseball was too tempting to resist. Jim quit school.

Although he never did get a diploma, Jim returned home in June and joined his 17 graduating classmates for the ceremonies, receiving a special certificate. And every fall, when he returned to his hometown, he always visited the school and advised students to finish their education.

4

COMING OF AGE

The train taking Connie Mack and the pitchers and catchers to Florida left Philadelphia on Friday evening, February 20th. Jim Foxx boarded the train at Baltimore with pitchers Eddie Rommel and Art Stokes, and another rookie, Lefty Grove. On the train they met a third rookie, Mickey Cochrane.

When Jim stepped off the train in Ft. Myers, Florida, two days later, he entered a world as different from Sudlersville as if he had landed on the moon.

Hundreds of people were at the station to greet the A's and a brass band blared a welcome. As the small group of players walked to the Grand Central Hotel, Jim noticed that many of the men about town wore knickers, loosely fitting trousers gathered at the knee, and colorful knee-high stockings. Before they broke camp, most of the A's would be sporting them, including Jim, who would become one of baseball's most dapper dressers.

The Philadelphia Athletics pose with Thomas Edison in 1927 on the porch of his home in Ft. Myers, Florida.

On Monday morning the A's went to the county fairgrounds in a motorbus for their first workout. The practice field was in the center of an oval race track, right in the middle of the Lee County Fair. The rest of the grounds were covered with a carnival midway. Animal acts and trapeze artists performed beside the diamond while the players did their best to concentrate on their practice games.

The focus of attention was on the two high-priced rookies, Lefty Grove and Mickey Cochrane. Grove, the strikeout king at Baltimore in the International League, had cost the A's $100,600, then the most money ever paid for a minor-league player. Cochrane, a former college football star, was the speediest catcher in baseball. He had hit

Foxx with teammates Mickey Cochrane and Al Simmons (left to right). Between them, the three future Hall of Famers hit more than 1,000 home runs.

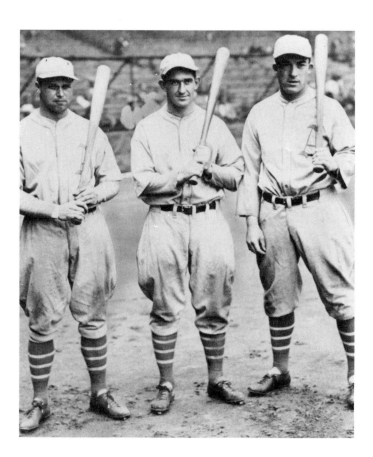

.350 at Portland, Oregon, and Connie Mack had paid $50,000 for him.

Jim, the youngest player in camp, was almost overshadowed by the others—but not for long. When he told teammate Al Simmons he had hit home runs at Easton that went farther than the palm trees ringing the field, Simmons thought he was only bragging. "Son," he said, "we play with baseballs, not golf balls, in this league." The next afternoon Foxx hit two over the trees.

Jim's speed and power did not go unnoticed by Connie Mack. One day a group of reporters came up to the manager and began raving about Cochrane.

"Yes," agreed Mack, "I think I landed a great player in Cochrane. But standing over there is the boy that attracts my eye."

The puzzled reporters looked where Mack was pointing.

"There he is," Mack went on. "That big young-ster warming up the pitchers. His name is Jimmie Foxx. He's the dandy of them all. He's going to be the greatest player in the land someday. He may not look like so much to you fellows now. He's green and lacks experience, and he doesn't know how to handle himself. But if I ever saw a diamond in the rough, it's that lad. And he is fast. He looks like a little truck, but he gets over the ground."

Impressed as Mack was with Foxx's potential, he knew the young rookie was not yet ready to play regularly in the majors. So when the 1925 season opened, Foxx found himself on the bench watching and learning. The inactivity made him restless. He wondered if he would be sent home, and worried about gaining weight.

Foxx finally got a chance to show what he could do, against the reigning world champion Washington Senators.With the A's trailing 9–4 in the 8th inning, Connie Mack sent Foxx in to pinch-hit for Lefty Grove. On a 2-2 count, Jim lined a base hit to left field for the first of his eventual 2,646 major-league hits.

Midway through the season, Mack decided that what Jim really needed was the chance to play every day, so he optioned him to Providence in the AAA International League. Playing third base and the outfield as well as catching, Foxx had a good two months there. When the Athletics recalled him on August 31, he was batting .327, although he had missed several games after dislocating his shoulder sliding into base.

Jim pinch-hit nine times for the year and came through with six hits. In one game he tried to score on a close play at home; nursing his sore shoulder, he did not slide and was called out. The newspapers gave him a roasting for his lack of hustle, but Jim did not let it upset him. He admitted that not sliding was an error of judgment on his part, and let it go at that.

After the Athletics finished the season a disappointing second behind Washington, Foxx went home to work on the family farm and do a little hunting.

Foxx stayed with the Athletics in 1926, but did not see much action. In 32 times at bat he hit .313 as the A's dropped to third place in the American League.

Although the A's improved in 1927, they finished 19 games behind the Yankees, who won an A.L. record 110 games. Foxx played in 61 games at first base and batted .323. The highlight of the year for him was his first major-league home run. He hit it at Philadelphia's Shibe Park on May 31st off the Yankees' veteran spitballer, Urban Shocker. Years

later, shortly after hitting his 500th homer, Foxx told reporters, "I remember more about the first homer I ever hit, because I was just a boy, and it meant something to me."

By the spring of 1928, it was obvious that Connie Mack would have to find a place in the lineup for Foxx to swing his bat every day. Although Foxx did play 20 games behind the plate, Cochrane had already established himself as the regular catcher (he was voted the league's Most Valuable Player that year). So Foxx alternated the season between third base (61 games) and first (30 games). Despite all that switching around in the field, there was one place Foxx always felt at home: the plate. He finished the season with a .328 average and 13 home runs, while the A's were once again second to the Yanks. Foxx was busy during the offseason as well. The day after Christmas, 1928, he eloped with Helen Heite, a young woman from Dover, Delaware, he had met and courted.

When the 1929 season opened, Connie Mack handed Foxx a first baseman's mitt and told him the position was his. With that move the A's began a three-year reign as the best team in baseball and Jimmie Foxx began a span of 14

Considered the most beautiful park in the major leagues when it was built in 1909, Shibe Park was home to the Philadelphia Athletics until 1955, when the team moved to Kansas City.

Jimmie Foxx with Connie Mack. Mack managed the A's for 50 years and was one of the last managers to wear street clothes in the dugout.

years as the league's most-feared slugger.

As a regular Foxx was hitting over .400 on June 1st. During one stretch he collected 3 hits every day for 6 days. He wound up with a .354 batting average and 33 home runs in 1929, the first of 12 consecutive years he would hit 30 or more. And with 117 RBIs, he began a 13-year streak driving in 100 or more runs. Nobody has ever matched those records of consistency. Thanks in large part to Foxx's firepower, the Athletics finally outplayed the Yanks for the A.L. pennant and the chance to meet the Chicago Cubs in the 1929 World Series.

Game 4 of the Series provided the usually placid young first baseman with his most anxious moment at bat. Trailing 8–0 in the last of the 7th, the A's had just staged the greatest rally in Series history. They had batted around and were within one run of tying the score when Foxx came to the plate with Cochrane on second and Simmons on first.

"There was moisture on my hands and on the back of my neck," Foxx later admitted. "Sheriff Blake, the Chicago pitcher, seemed to be a little man standing far off at the small end of a telescope.

"'Well, Foxx,' I said to myself, 'get in there. You either do or you don't.' I took a deep breath and swung at one of Blake's slants and drove a single to center. Mickey was off like a demon, rounding third and tearing for home before I reached first base. [Jimmy] Dykes then drove in two more runs with a double. When I reached the bench, Connie Mack looked at me and said, 'Nice work, boy. You got the big hit.'

"I have always felt the force of that advice I gave myself in that game: you either do or you don't. Following it, I simply try to pick out a good ball and whale away at it. If I connect, it's apt to be important. If I don't, I have some satisfaction from the fact that I was trying, at least."

Foxx had another reason to feel satisfied as the A's beat the Cubs, 4 games to 1. His winning World Series share in 1929 was $5,620.57, doubling his income for the year. Along with most players of the day, he put much of his money into the stock market, which had been going up, up, up, just like a Foxx home run. He was counting on his investments to secure his financial future.

Jimmie Foxx was on top of the world. His first son, James Emory Foxx, Jr., was born on October 3, the same day the Cubs won their only World Series game. But within a few weeks of the A's big victory, the stock market crashed and the Great Depression started. Foxx lost every penny he had invested.

The Athletics repeated as world champions in 1930, this time defeating the St. Louis Cardinals. Foxx used some of his $5,785 winner's share for a down payment on a farm for his parents, but the Depression got worse and they eventually lost it.

Following the 1930 season, Foxx signed a three-year contract for $50,000—just under $17,000 a year. Although he slumped to .291 with 30 home runs in 1931, the A's won another pennant. This time, though, they lost the Series to the Cards.

Foxx was well known for his generosity to others. He always tipped the clubhouse boy who ran errands for him, along with the waiters and porters and hotel bellboys who had a tough time squeezing a dime out of most players. Foxx also gave his brother several thousand dollars every

In game 1 of the 1929 World Series, Foxx scores the first run after hitting a home run into the center-field bleachers.

year, and his father could count on him whenever he needed cash to sow the spring crops. Moreover, Foxx enjoyed night clubs and restaurants, and was an avid check-grabber.

His generosity even extended to opposing players. One day in Chicago, Foxx was waiting to take infield practice while rookie Billy Sullivan, Jr, who had just reported to the White Sox from Notre Dame, was working out at first.

"When I was finished," Sullivan later recalled, "I threw my glove on the ground, the way we did in those days. Foxx picked it up. As I was walking away, he called me over. 'We don't use gloves like this up here,' he said. 'It's too small.'

"I told him it was the only one I could find in South Bend. The next day he came out with two gloves. He handed me one that was all broken in just right and said, 'Take it, it's yours.'"

Foxx displays an MVP cup, one of three MVP awards the big slugger won. He also finished second to Joe DiMaggio in the 1939 MVP voting.

and there's no telling how many more he might have collected if opposing pitchers had not walked him 116 times.

Even so, no righthanded hitter has ever hit more home runs in a season than Jimmie Foxx did in 1932. Along with his league-leading 169 RBIs and .364 average, they were more than enough to earn him the American League's Most Valuable Player award.

By 1933, the Depression had hit Philadelphia hard. It was an industrial city and unemployment there was even higher than the 25 percent national rate. The A's' attendance, which reached a high of 839,000 in 1929, fell to 297,000 in just four years. Hard-pressed banks were calling in loans. Connie Mack owed them $400,000. To make his payments, the club owner was forced to sell some of his stars.

The A's slipped to third in 1933, but Foxx remained hot. On July 2nd he hit 2 homers in the first game of a doubleheader at St. Louis; in the second he hit 2 more, plus a double and a triple. Then, on August 14th, he set a league record by contributing 9 RBIs to an 11–5 win at Cleveland. Those were just a few high points in an outstanding season that ended up with a .356 average, 48 home runs, and 163 RBIs for Foxx—all tops in the league. And once again he was named MVP.

That same year, the first All-Star game was played in Chicago, and Foxx was elected to the American League team. He would play in seven All-Star games, at third base and first, during his long career.

Unfortunately, Foxx reached his peak playing and earning years at the wrong time and in the wrong place. The Great Depression, the Athletics' fading fortunes, and the dwindling fans had a greater effect on his earnings than his two super seasons. When his contract expired at the end of 1933, the A's offered him $11,000, a 30 percent cut. By threatening to remain in Sudlersville, he finally managed to get the figure up to $18,000— about half what Babe Ruth, then 40 years old, was earning.

Mack continued to sell his other stars to keep the A's in business. Foxx, at the age of 26, started 1934 as the senior man on the team. Although he had another fine season (44 homers, 130 RBIs, and a .334 batting average), the team finished way down in fifth place.

Connie Mack had been unable to find an adequate replacement for Mickey Cochrane. So, in the spring of 1935, he asked Foxx to become a catcher again. It was a drastic move, switching the game's top slugger to a position he had not played regularly for six years. Foxx was concerned that it would affect his hitting, as the catcher's chores take more out of a player than any other position. But he was willing to do whatever Mack thought best for the team. In fact, before his long career finally ended in 1945, Foxx would play every position except second base.

"Foxxie [or *Fawksie*, as Connie Mack pronounced the name] is the easiest boy on the team to handle," the manager said. "He does whatever I ask him to do, with never a word of complaint."

Although Foxx had never been a very graceful first baseman, he had worked hard and developed into a dependable fielder. In his first full year he made just 7 errors, and rarely made many more than 10 a season. He was adept at charging a bunt and throwing righthanded. As a catcher, however, he was much less effective, and after 26 games Mack moved him back to first.

In the 1935 All-Star game Foxx drove in 3 runs to lead the American League to a 4–1 victory. Gomez, the winning pitcher, was happy to find himself on Foxx's side.

Foxx finished out the season with a .346 average and 36 home runs (tops in the league), but the A's wound up at the bottom, with a dismal 58-91 record.

6

THE BOSTON BOOM

Tom Yawkey, owner of the Boston Red Sox, had the desire—and the money—to build a winning team. He had already bought Lefty Grove and Rube Walberg from the A's, and in December 1935 he paid Connie Mack $150,000 for Jimmie Foxx and pitcher Johnny Marcum.

Foxx began his 12th major-league season in a new uniform, but otherwise he looked pretty much the same—as fast and powerful as ever. His 1936 stats included a .338 average and 41 home runs. Though he did not capture any batting titles that year, a dahlia named in his honor won three prizes at the annual flower show of the American Dahlia Society. The Jimmie Foxx dahlia was a huge coppery-red flower, more than a foot in diameter. A new addition in Foxx's life was his second son, William Kenneth, born in May 1936. A third son, James Emory Foxx III, would be born in 1944.

Foxx hits home run number 495 against Washington on August 16, 1940, to win the game in the 10th inning. Catching is another future Hall of Famer, Rick Ferrell.

Foxx's 1937 output would have been considered excellent for any other player: a .285 batting average, 36 home runs, 127 RBIs; but for him it was a fearful slump. Sinus problems caused his eyes to water and tight pain to thump in his head. Some people began to wonder whether Foxx was over the hill at 29.

But Foxx was not finished yet. He bounced right back in 1938 with 50 home runs, a league-leading 175 RBIs, and a league-leading .349 average, almost single-handedly pulling the Sox up from 5th place to 2nd. That performance earned him his third Most Valuable Player trophy. It also brought him a contract for $27,000, plus another $5,000 in bonuses, the most he had ever made.

In the spring of 1939, Jimmie Foxx met rookie Ted Williams, a cocky kid who thought he was the greatest hitter the world had ever seen—not without justification. For the next few years the pair formed the most powerful one-two punch since Ruth and Lou Gehrig. An intense student of hitting, Williams watched his super-slugging teammate closely. Whenever Foxx drove one over the fence in batting practice, Williams would exclaim to anyone around him, "Holy Pete, did you see that one go!"

Williams—and the rest of Foxx's many fans—got 35 opportunities to see their hero's home runs go in 1939. Foxx's batting average soared to .360 that season, and he finished second to Joe DiMaggio in the MVP balloting.

Although it was his hitting that brought Foxx fame, he always felt that he could pitch better than a lot of the men he faced. He got his first chance to prove it one day in Boston after the Tigers had pounded every Red Sox hurler in sight. In desper-ation, manager Joe Cronin asked Foxx to move from first base to the mound. Foxx

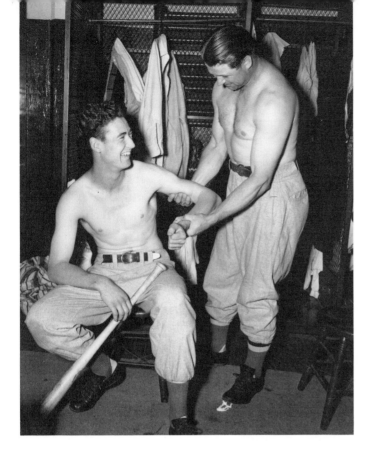

Foxx checks the muscles of the young slugger Ted Williams, who first joined the Red Sox as a brash 20-year-old in the 1939 spring training camp. Williams later said of Foxx, "Next to Joe DiMaggio, he was the greatest player I ever saw."

happily obliged—and pitched one perfect inning.

Still, his greatest moments came against opposing pitchers. On August 16, 1940, Foxx passed two milestones when he hit 2 home runs against Washington. With the first one, number 30 of the season, he became the only player to hit 30 or more in 12 consecutive seasons; and with the second one he passed Lou Gehrig's career total of 493. Then on September 24th, he reached another major mark. In a game against his old teammates, he became the second player to rack up 500 home runs. The big blast came in the midst of a Boston blitz against the Athletics and received little attention.

Twenty-five years later Foxx told a writer he was unaware of its significance at the time, and could not even recall who was pitching.

"I'll tell you what I remember about it," he said. "I remember that it was hit in the same park that I hit my first homer, Shibe Park. And I remember that after I hit it, [Boston outfielder] Doc Cramer... somehow retrieved the ball and gave it to me.

"'Jimmie,' he said, 'you ought to keep this. It's your five hundredth home run.' Until then, I didn't know, because the press didn't make any fuss about it. After all, Babe Ruth hit 714."

But it was not mere numbers that moved Boston *Times-Herald* writer Buck O'Neill to nominate Jimmie Foxx as the greatest of all ballplayers. Ty Cobb was great, he wrote. Ruth was mighty. But it was in team spirit that "Jimmie Foxx stands out above all others...."

The occasion for that tribute came when Boston catcher Gene Desautels went into a batting slump. Although he had not put on the shinguards for five years, Foxx volunteered to do the catching to get more punch in the lineup, and he caught 42 games in six weeks.

Foxx's batting average dropped to .297 and

Foxx chats with Yankees slugger Lou Gehrig before the start of the 1939 season. Gehrig, sick with an incurable disease, took himself out of the lineup on May 2nd after playing 2,130 consecutive games.

.300 in 1940 and 1941, respectively, and his 1941 RBI total of 105 was the second time he had so few since becoming such a dominant hitter. Yet one of those RBI's had a very special meaning for him:

On July 26, 1941, Lefty Grove, one of the rookies Foxx had met on the train to Florida in 1925, was at the end of his career. He had tried several times to chalk up his 300th win, a goal all pitchers dream of reaching. Grove was locked in a 6–6 tie with the Indians when Foxx came to the plate with two men on base and came through with a booming triple to win the game—Grove's 300th and final victory.

7

BACK TO PHILADELPHIA

Foxx got off to a slow start in 1942, and after 30 games was batting only .270. The Red Sox put him on waivers, which meant that any team could claim him, and on June 1st he was picked up by the Chicago Cubs.

Just before he left the Red Sox, Foxx was hit by a pitch that broke two ribs. When he got to Chicago he was taped tightly, and he expected to have a few weeks to recover. But even though he could not swing the bat properly and was no threat at the plate, three days later he was pressed into action.

The Cubs thought his eyes were bothering him; the doctor blamed a sinus condition. Whatever the cause, Foxx never did regain his power at the plate. He batted .205 and hit just 3 home runs.

In a game against the Giants, he put on the catching gear again. His first time at bat, a pitch coming out of the white shirts in the center-field bleachers went right past his head.

When the Giants came to bat, one of them said to Foxx, "Jimmie, why don't you get out of here? You're going to get killed."

Foxx laughed and said, "I got to eat, don't I?"

Playing for the Chicago Cubs, Foxx displays his round-house swing. Foxx led the league in strikeouts 7 times.

In fact, Foxx could not afford to quit. He was broke. Realizing his playing days would end soon, he had invested some of his earnings in leases on two Florida golf courses. But before he could use his options to buy the properties, World War II broke out and the government took over the sites. His losses were increased when his partners disappeared with $30,000. He was hanging on in Chicago, doing the only thing he knew.

Foxx was out of baseball for all of 1943, then came back the next season as a coach and occasional player for the Cubs. In August 1944 they asked him to finish the year managing their farm team in Portsmouth, Virginia. Foxx did not like managing, however. It was easier to hit home runs, he decided, than it was to handle 17 other players who thought they were home-run hitters.

Cut loose at the end of the year, the 37-year-old Foxx was not yet ready to retire. Although he weighed 200 pounds, he believed his legs and eyes were still sound. Many of the best pitchers had left the game to serve in the military, and Foxx felt that he could hit wartime pitching. The Philadelphia Blue Jays, as the Phillies were called in 1944 and 1945, had lost their first baseman to the navy, and they agreed. They signed Foxx. Playing first and third for them in 1945, he hit a respectable .268 with 7 home runs.

But the highlight of the year came when Foxx finally got his chance to be a starting pitcher. It was in a war-relief exhibition game against the Athletics, and Foxx pitched three scoreless innings before he tired and was knocked out in the 4th.

The Blue Jays used him in relief a few times after that and then started him in the second game of a doubleheader at home against the Reds on August 19th. Using a fastball and screwball, Foxx

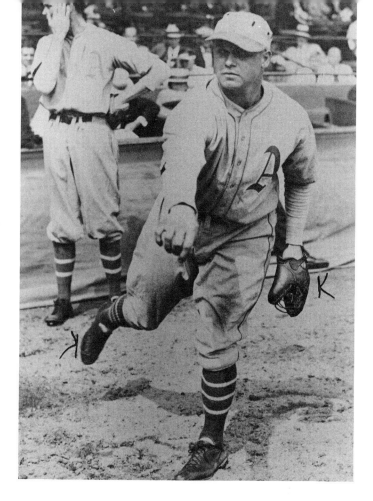

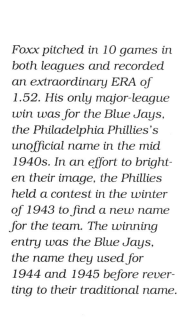

Foxx pitched in 10 games in both leagues and recorded an extraordinary ERA of 1.52. His only major-league win was for the Blue Jays, the Philadelphia Phillies's unofficial name in the mid 1940s. In an effort to brighten their image, the Phillies held a contest in the winter of 1943 to find a new name for the team. The winning entry was the Blue Jays, the name they used for 1944 and 1945 before reverting to their traditional name.

gave up just one hit in the first six innings and had a 4–1 lead. But then, with two out in the 7th, the Reds got three straight hits, and Blue Jays manager Ben Chapman took him out. Walking off the field, Foxx was given as loud an ovation as he had ever received for one of his mammoth home runs. Relief pitcher Andy Karl held on to the lead, and Foxx was credited with his one and only major-league victory as a pitcher.

The next day he was back at first base again. Although he hit his fifth home run of the season in the 8th inning, the Reds showed their disdain for the aging slugger by intentionally walking a pitcher to get to him. That was their mistake. With the bases loaded, Foxx came up and hit a long fly over the outfielders to drive in the winning runs. Though only 950 fans were there to see it, that may have been one of the most satisfying hits of Jimmie Foxx's great career. But it was not the last.

Before retiring at the end of the season, Foxx went out with an echo of the thunder of his youth. On September 9th in Pittsburgh he hit a home run in the first of two games. He was 4 for 5 including his last home run, and had 5 RBIs in the Blue Jays' 14–3 nightcap victory. To top it all off, he collected two more hits the next day and a double the day after.

The Blue Jays played another doubleheader at Brooklyn on September 23rd. Playing first base in the second game, Foxx hit a double off the Dodgers'

Catcher Jimmie with his brother Sammy during the spring training period in Florida. Sammy never played in the major leagues.

Tom Seats and contributed 2 RBIs to the Blue Jays'
4–3 win. It was fitting that his last hit should drive
in the winning runs for his team. That was what
Jimmie Foxx liked most to do, whether he was
playing for the world champion Philadelphia Athletics or the last-place Philadelphia Blue Jays.

8

IN TRIBUTE

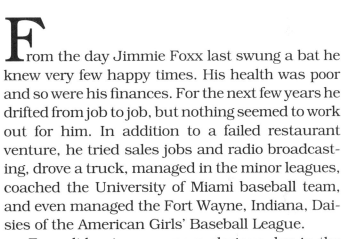

From the day Jimmie Foxx last swung a bat he knew very few happy times. His health was poor and so were his finances. For the next few years he drifted from job to job, but nothing seemed to work out for him. In addition to a failed restaurant venture, he tried sales jobs and radio broadcasting, drove a truck, managed in the minor leagues, coached the University of Miami baseball team, and even managed the Fort Wayne, Indiana, Daisies of the American Girls' Baseball League.

Foxx did enjoy one more glorious day in the spotlight, however. In the summer of 1951, he was inducted into baseball's Hall of Fame at Cooperstown, New York.

Foxxie's old manager, Connie Mack, was there to congratulate him. Never much of a speechmaker, Foxx humbly accepted his plaque with these words: "All the years I played, all the great players I saw, played against, read about and watched, there

Foxx was coach for the Minneapolis Millers, the Red Sox's top minor-league team. Lu Clinton (right) and Pumpsie Green, both of whom would play for the Red Sox, look on as Jimmie demonstrates his home-run swing.

always seemed to be so many great players. I never expected this honor. I'll never forget it."

Recalling his 1932 attempt to break Babe Ruth's record, Foxx explained that much as he would have liked to break it, he would not have minded if someone else had topped him in turn.

"I think it's always better for fans if they know the players who set records. They have someone to go out and cheer for. I think it would be a good thing if someone broke Ruth's record now."

And true to his word, Foxx had nothing but good wishes for Willie Mays when he socked his 535th home run in 1966 to pass Foxx in the record books. In fact, Foxx said he was rooting for Mays to reach 600.

While he cheered others on, Foxx's own life continued to decline. First he suffered a heart attack; and then a fall inflicted a fractured skull and spinal injuries. He was not eligible for a baseball pension since those benefits were only put into effect after Foxx retired. Fortunately, however, Foxx had been a member of the Association of Professional Ball Players for 20 years and received some money from that group. He also drew Social Security disability income after his heart attack.

When the Boston baseball writers invited him to their annual winter banquet in 1958, Foxx was living in Miami and did not have the money to make the trip. Once this was revealed, offers of help and jobs came to him, but his health did not permit him to work.

Through it all, Foxx blamed nobody but himself. "I had pride, but pride's not much good when you're flat broke," he said. "I blew a lot of dough, and that's my fault. When you've been up and come down, a lot of people don't know you exist anymore.

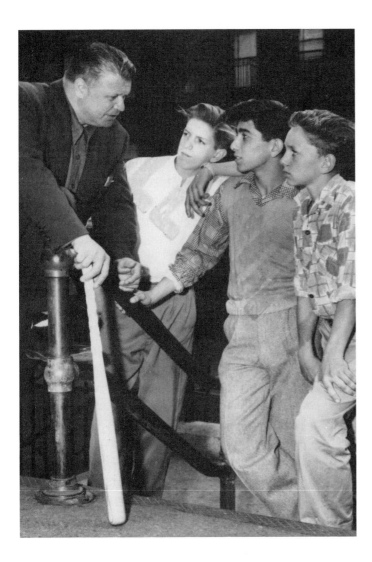

After his retirement, Jimmie worked with youngsters in New York City in 1954 to help fight juvenile delinquency.

And a lot more think you've got a million dollars."

But broke as he was, Foxx remained the same warm-hearted, generous person he had always been. And as it turned out, he still had a lot to give. As a young boy, Gil Dunn, a pharmacist on Kent Island in Chesapeake Bay, had idolized Foxx. Dunn began to collect photos and newspaper clippings and memorabilia about Foxx to display in his pharmacy. When Foxx heard about it, he decided to pay this fan a visit.

"One day in 1966," Dunn recalled, "this big, burly, white-haired man walked into my store. It was Jimmie Foxx. I was speechless. He unloaded the trunk of his car and gave me everything in it: a Boston uniform, small flat old gloves, caps, plaques, photos, and a uniform. I know he could have sold those things, and I'm sure he needed the money, but he just gave them to me. He as much as told me I might as well have the things, as I seemed to care."

Less than a year later, on July 21, 1967, Jimmie Foxx was eating dinner at his brother's home in Miami. A piece of meat got stuck in his throat and he choked. Before help could arrive, he was dead, at age 59.

Jimmie Foxx had been mistaken when he said a lot of people did not know he existed anymore. Gil Dunn knew. All of his Foxx memorabilia is still on view today in the Kent Island Pharmacy. The people of Sudlersville knew, too. On October 24, 1987, the town's Community Betterment Club dedicated a memorial to him. It stands right at the intersection where the first electric light bulb was illuminated in the year young Jim was named the state's outstanding schoolboy athlete.

The monument to Foxx in Sudlersville, Maryland.

A fan named George Clader wrote to the committee from Texas: "I grew up in Philadelphia. From 1929 to 1933, I saved every penny in my lunch money while in junior high and high school to go to Shibe Park to see the A's. I saw Jimmie Foxx hit many home runs. Nobody hit them so often or so far....To say he was my idol is putting it mildly....Anyone who saw Foxxie hit one of his long-distance shots can never forget him. I am 70 now, and to me he was the most exciting player I ever saw."

It was not just the fans who appreciated Foxx. Although he was unable to attend the service, Ted Williams—himself one of the greatest hitters in baseball history—sent this letter to Sudlersville:

"I'll never forget my old teammate and how nicely he treated me as a young brash rookie, and what an impression he made on me when I first saw him hit. I don't believe anyone ever made the impact of the ball and bat sound like he did when he really got ahold of it.

"He was born in farm country; I don't think he ever really left it. He was as down to earth as anyone I ever met. I remember as a rookie the great Jimmie hitting ahead of me and he crushed one against the wind at Fenway [Park]. As I shook his hand at home plate he made me feel weak when he gripped my hand.

"He was affectionately called The Beast because of his strength, and no one felt so lost when he left the Red Sox in 1942 as I. I loved him. I know all his friends miss him as surely as I do."

Jimmie Foxx surely was missed, but he was also remembered. His legendary feats live on in the memories of his many fans—and in the record books.

CHRONOLOGY

Oct. 22, 1907	Born James Emory Foxx in Sudlersville, Maryland.
May 1923	Named outstanding schoolboy athlete in Maryland.
May 1924	Signs with Easton Farmers of Eastern Shore League.
Aug. 1924	Sold to Philadelphia Athletics for $2,500.
May 1, 1925	Makes first of 2,646 major-league hits.
Dec. 26, 1928	Elopes with and marries Helen Heite.
Oct. 3, 1929	James Emory Foxx, Jr. is born.
1932	Hits 58 home runs, a record for righthanded batters; wins American League's MVP award.
June 7-8, 1933	Ties major-league record with 4 home runs in 4 times at bat.
July 2, 1933	Ties major-league record with 4 home runs in doubleheader.
Aug. 14, 1933	Sets A.L. single-game record with 9 RBIs.
1933	Wins American League triple crown and second MVP award.
Dec. 10, 1935	Sold to Boston Red Sox.
May 25, 1936	William Kenneth Foxx is born.
1938	Wins third MVP award; leads A.L. in batting.
1940	Hits 30 or more home runs for 12th consecutive year.
1941	Drives in 100 or more runs for 13th consecutive year.
June 1, 1942	Sold to Chicago Cubs.
1944	James Emory Foxx III born.
Aug. 19, 1945	Wins first—and last—major-league decision as a pitcher.
Sept. 9, 1945	Hits 534th home run, the last in his career.
1951	Elected to the Baseball Hall of Fame.
July 21, 1967	Dies in Miami, Florida.

JAMES E.(JIMMY) FOXX
PHILADELPHIA(A.L.)1926-35
BOSTON(A.L.)1936-42;CHICAGO(N.L.)1942-44
PHILADELPHIA(N.L.)1945

NOTED FOR HIS BATTING,PARTICULARLY AS A
HOME RUN HITTER.COLLECTED 534 HOME RUNS
IN 2,317 GAMES.HAD A LIFETIME BATTING
AVERAGE OF.325 AND,IN THREE WORLD
SERIES.COMPILED A MARK OF.344.APPEARED
IN SEVEN ALL STAR GAMES IN WHICH HE
BATTED.316.PLAYED FIRST AND THIRD BASES
AND ALSO WAS A CATCHER.

MAJOR LEAGUE STATISTICS

Philadelphia A's, Boston Red Sox, Chicago Cubs, Philadelphia Phillies

Year	Team	G	AB	R	H	2B	3B	HR	RBI	AVG	SB
1925	PHI A	10	9	2	6	1	0	0	0	.667	0
1926		26	32	8	10	2	1	0	5	.313	1
1927		61	130	23	42	6	5	3	29	.323	2
1928		118	400	85	131	29	10	13	79	.328	3
1929		149	517	123	183	23	9	33	117	.354	10
1930		153	562	127	188	33	13	37	156	.335	7
1931		139	515	93	150	32	10	30	120	.291	4
1932		154	585	151	213	33	9	58	169	.364	3
1933		149	573	125	204	37	9	48	163	.356	2
1934		150	539	120	180	28	6	44	130	.334	11
1935		147	535	118	185	33	7	36	115	.346	6
1936	BOS A	155	585	130	198	32	8	41	143	.338	13
1937		150	569	111	162	24	6	36	127	.285	10
1938		149	565	139	197	33	9	50	175	.349	5
1939		124	467	130	168	31	10	35	105	.360	4
1940		144	515	106	153	30	4	36	119	.297	4
1941		135	487	87	146	27	8	19	105	.300	2
1942	2 team total BOS A (30G – .270) CHI N (70G – .205)										
		100	305	43	69	12	0	8	33	.226	1
1944	CHI N	15	20	0	1	1	0	0	2	.050	0
1945	PHI N	89	224	30	60	11	1	7	38	.268	0
Total		2317	8134	1751	2646	458	125	534	1921	.325	88

World Series
(3 years)

		18	64	11	22	3	1	4	11	.344	0

All-Star Games
(7 years)

		7	19	3	6	1	0	1	4	.316	0

Pitching record

Year	Team	W	L	PCT	ERA	G	GS	CG	IP	H	BB	SO	ShO
1939	BOS A	0	0	—	0.00	1	0	0	1	0	0	1	0
1945	PHI N	1	0	1.000	1.59	9	2	0	22.2	13	14	10	0
Total		1	0	1.000	1.52	10	2	0	23.2	13	14	11	0

FURTHER READING

Allen, Lee. *Kings of the Diamond.* New York: Putnam, 1965.

Astor, Gerald. *The Baseball Hall of Fame 50th Anniversary Book.* New York: Prentice-Hall, 1988.

Danzig, Allison, and Joe Reichler. *History of Baseball.* Englewood Cliffs, NJ: Prentice-Hall, 1959.

Honig, Donald. *Baseball America.* New York: Macmillan, 1986.

James, Bill. *Baseball Abstract.* New York: Ballantine, 1983.

Lieb, Frederick G. *Baseball Story.* New York: Putnam, 1950.

Lieb, Frederick G. *Connie Mack.* New York: Putnam, 1945.

Meany, Tom. *Baseball's Greatest Players.* New York: Grosset & Dunlap, 1953.

Pratt, John Lowell. *Baseball's All-Stars.* Garden City, NY: Doubleday, 1967.

Smith, Ira. *Baseball's Famous First Basemen.* New York: A.S. Barnes, 1954.

Thorn, John. *A Century of Baseball Lore.* New York: Hart Publishing, 1974.

INDEX

PICTURE CREDITS

AP/Wide World Photos: pp. 40, 50, 52; From the Collection of Gil Dunn: pp. 12, 14, 18, 30, 34, 37; National Baseball Library, Cooperstown, NY: pp. 2, 8, 21, 24, 26, 29, 44, 46, 49, 60; Sudlersville Memorial Library, Sudlersville, MD: p. 56; UPI/Bettmann: pp. 32, 43, 55, 58

NORMAN MACHT was a minor league general manager with the Milwaukee Braves and Baltimore Orioles organizations and has been a stock broker and college professor. His work has appeared in *The BallPlayers*, *The Sporting News*, *Baseball Digest* and *Sports Heritage*, and he is the co-author with Dick Bartell of *Rowdy Richard*. Norman Macht lives in Newark, Delaware.

JIM MURRAY, veteran sports columnist of the *Los Angeles Times*, is one of America's most acclaimed writers. He has been named "America's Best Sportswriter" by the National Association of Sportscasters and Sportswriters 14 times, was awarded the Red Smith Award, and was twice winner of the National Headliner Award. In addition, he was awarded the J. G. Taylor Spink Award in 1987 for "meritorious contributions to baseball writing." With this award came his 1988 induction into the National Baseball Hall of Fame in Cooperstown, New York. In 1990, Jim Murray was awarded the Pulitzer Prize for Commentary.

EARL WEAVER is the winningest manager in Baltimore Orioles history by a wide margin. He compiled 1,480 victories in his 17 years at the helm. After managing eight different minor league teams, he was given the chance to lead the Orioles in 1968. Under his leadership the Orioles finished lower than second place in the American League East only four times in 17 years. One of only 12 managers in big league history to have managed in four or more World Series, Earl was named Manager of the Year in 1979. The popular Weaver had his number 5 retired in 1982, joining Brooks Robinson, Frank Robinson, and Jim Palmer, whose numbers were retired previously. Earl Weaver continues his association with the professional baseball scene by writing, broadcasting, and coaching.